Making quilts really didn't start for me until we moved to Deadwood, Oregon from Berkeley just before Christmas of 1975. Before that, besides drawing, I was doing lots of embroideries, mostly using handspun yarn I got from Ralph Prince, who worked with my husband, Ernie, at the Berkeley Public Library.

From 1980 to 1990 I designed porcelain china for Block China of New York. When Jay Block died of a heart attack while running with his dog, another era came to an end. I decided to do a series of quilts that matched the china patterns for a show I would call "Eating Off Of and Sleeping Under."

Since Ernie died in 2004 my need to share my feelings about my grief and loss and my life now has been strong. This book is a way of sharing those feelings with some quilts I've made recently. And plus a few earlier ones that added a touch that was fun!

When I was fifteen I had a kind of epiphany at 4 o'clock one morning—not asleep but not really awake—of an utter void and nothingness, realizing I would never understand what life was, it would always be a mystery. But as long as I was in this world I would have projects. So here's my latest one.

Thank you to so many people (also my cat) for inspiring me. My parents Hulda and Willis Rich, my husband Ernie, son David, daughter Anya, son Jonevan, grandson Colins, brother Jim, sisters Carol and Suzanne, a multitude of friends, and now Laurie and Larry and Churpa for helping me put this quilt book together.

Also, thanks to the designers of the cloth in the quilts as well as people in the factories producing the cloth.

It connects me to the human family, what I've always wanted to do with my art— bring the human family closer together.

When 9/11 happened my first thought was holding hands with everyone on the planet in a giant circle.

The quilts are all made by hand with every stitch a prayer.

Mary Lou Goertzen

Purple Tulips 1992

Inspired by purple tulips my daughter brought me, I made sixteen different embroideries.

I needed help with how to present them and was fortunate to have help from my women's artist group in Eugene.

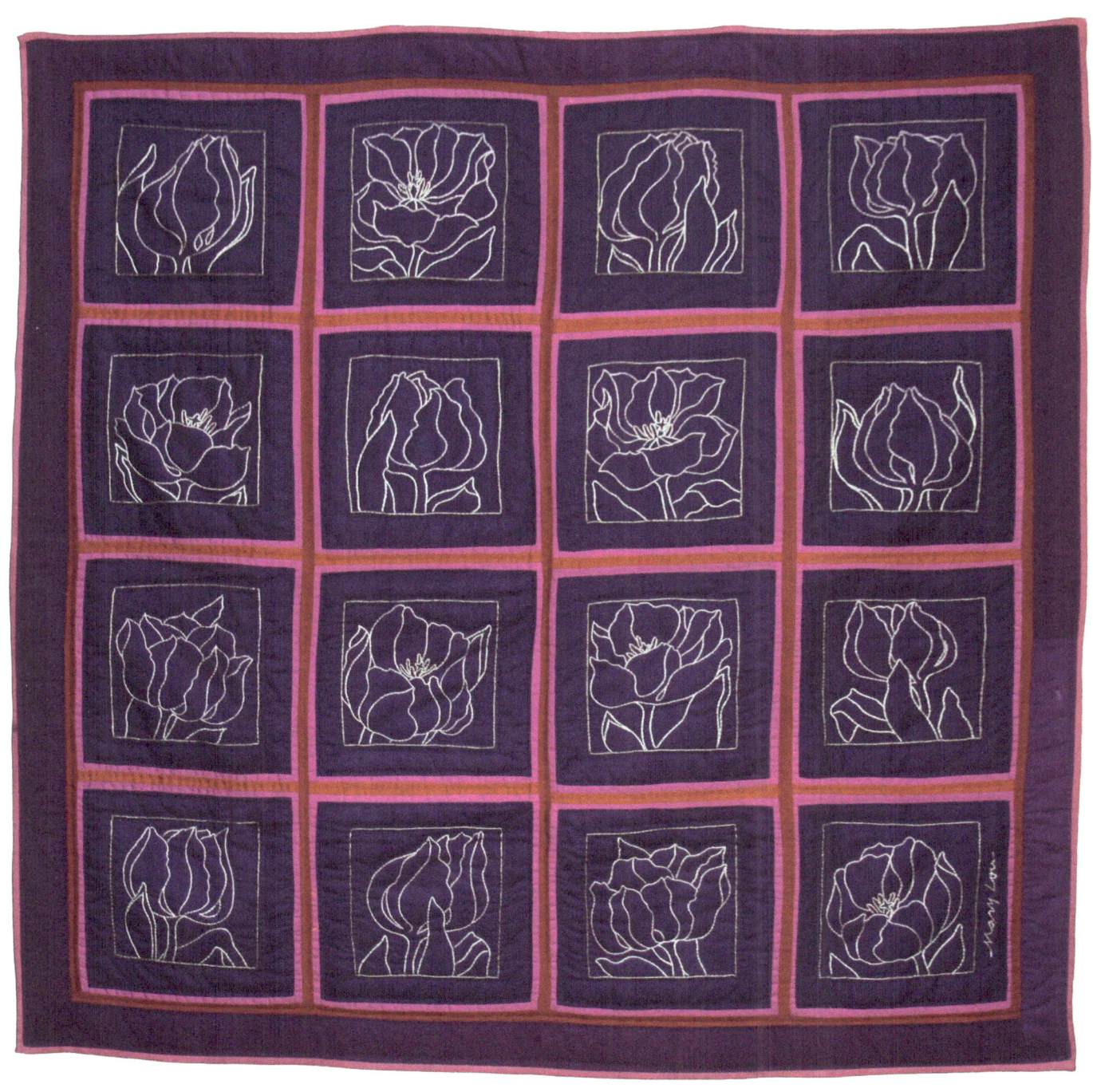

PURPLE TULIPS

Four Patch –
Trip to Kansas 1993

Since I enjoy keeping my hands busy, I cut out the four patches so I could sew in the car on a trip to Kansas.

It's a favorite of mine.

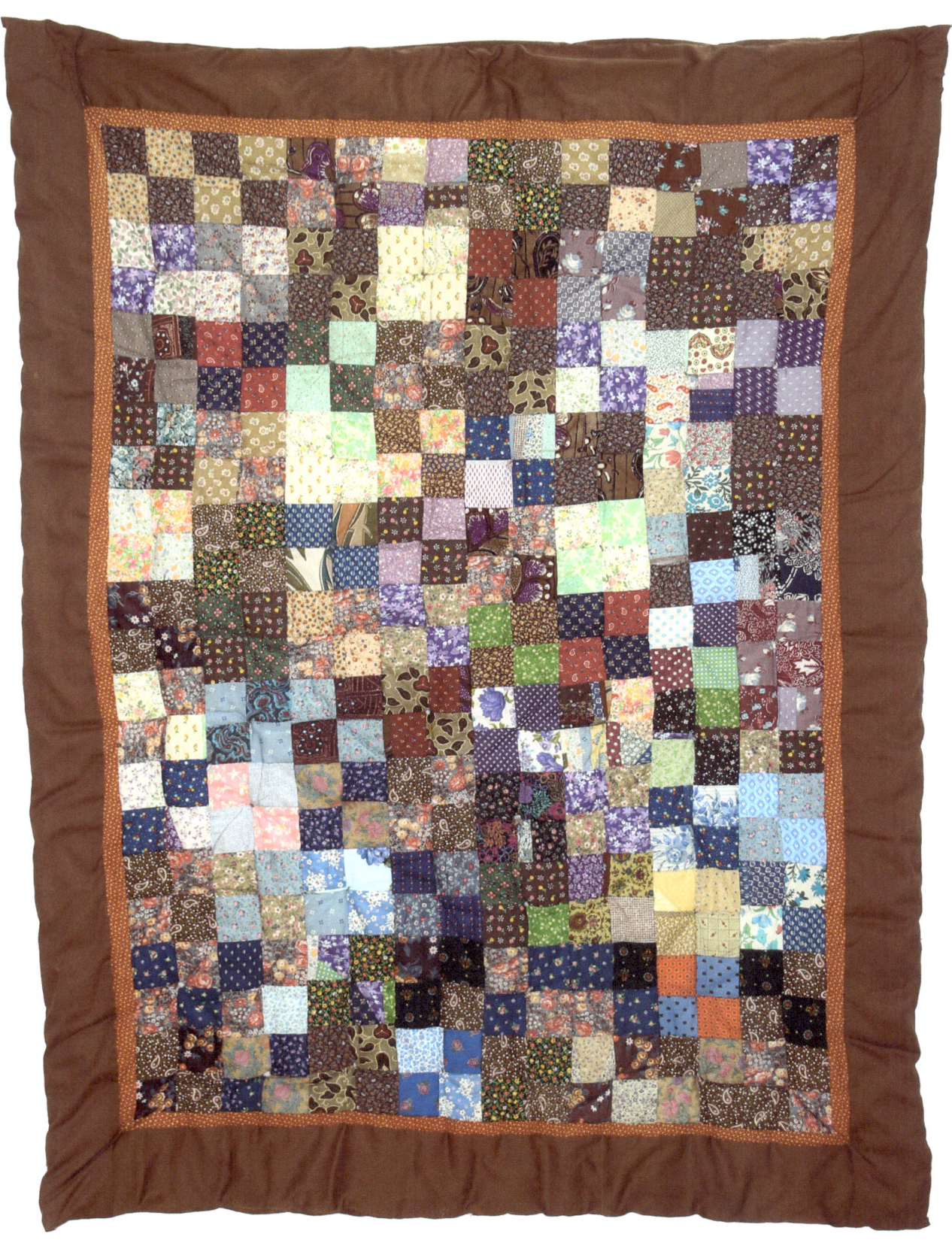

FOUR PATCH - TRIP TO KANSAS

Trillium   1994

After the porcelain china designing days were over I decided to celebrate the ten year era in my life by designing quilts that "matched" the china patterns.

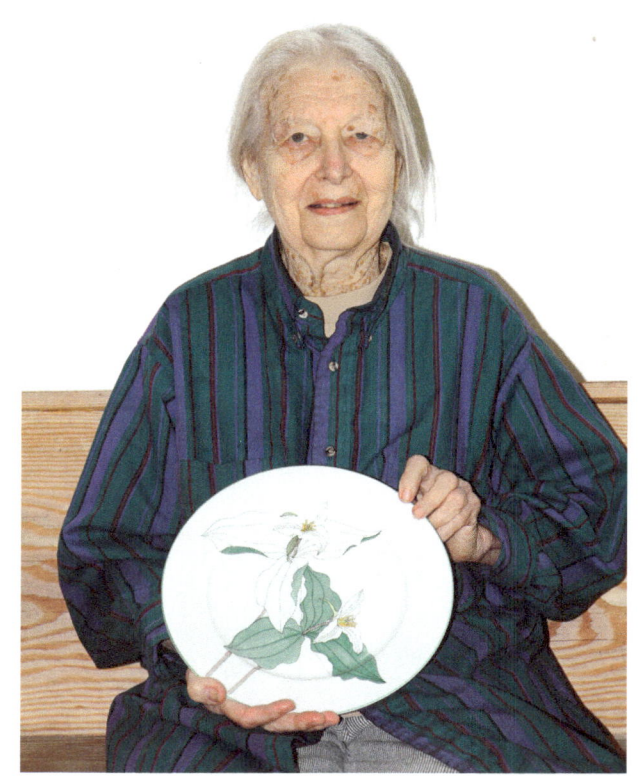

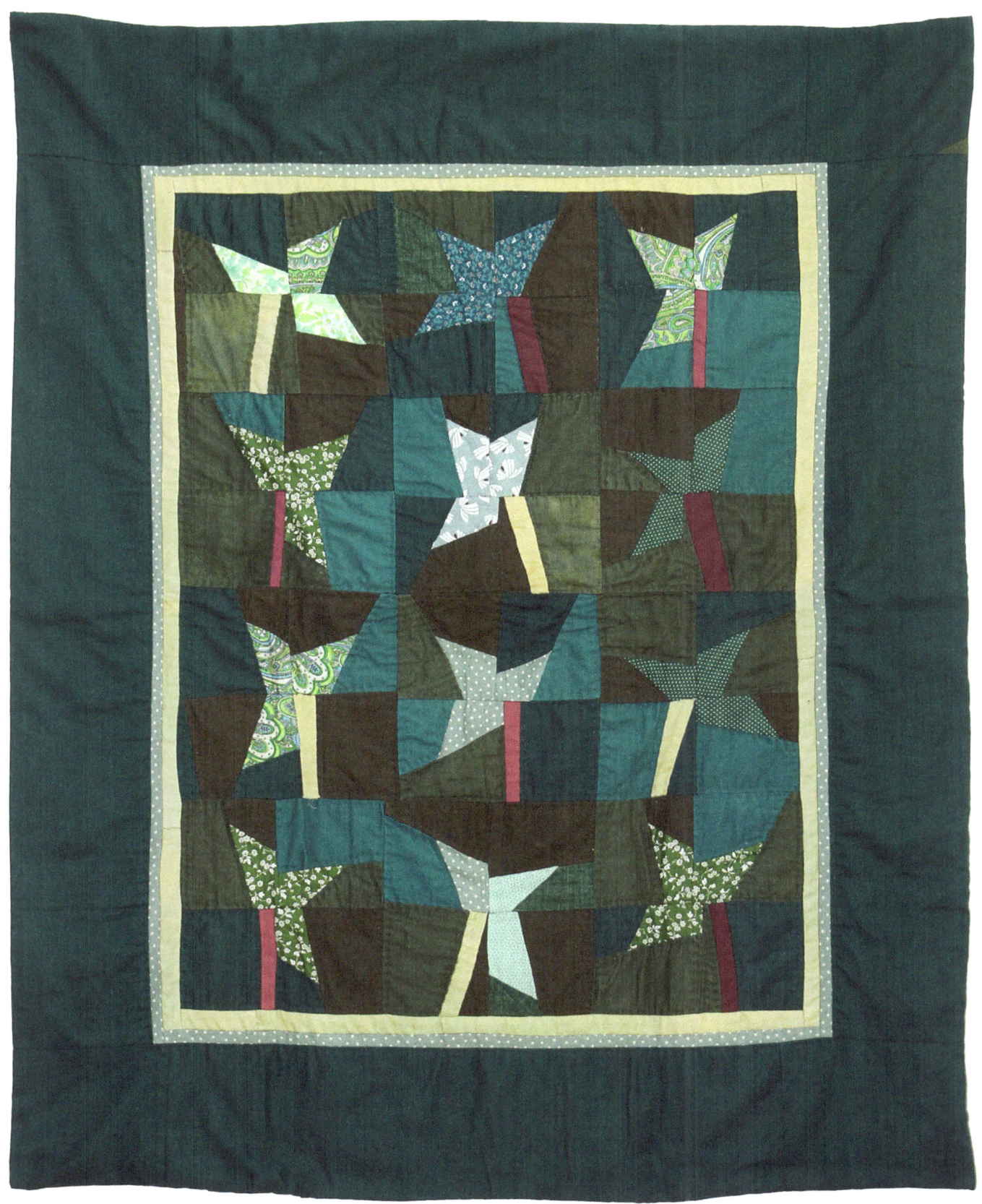

TRILLIUM

Hooray for Saturday Market
2012

Eugene Saturday Market
has been a very important
community in our family.
So many good connections
and stories through the years
since the 70's.

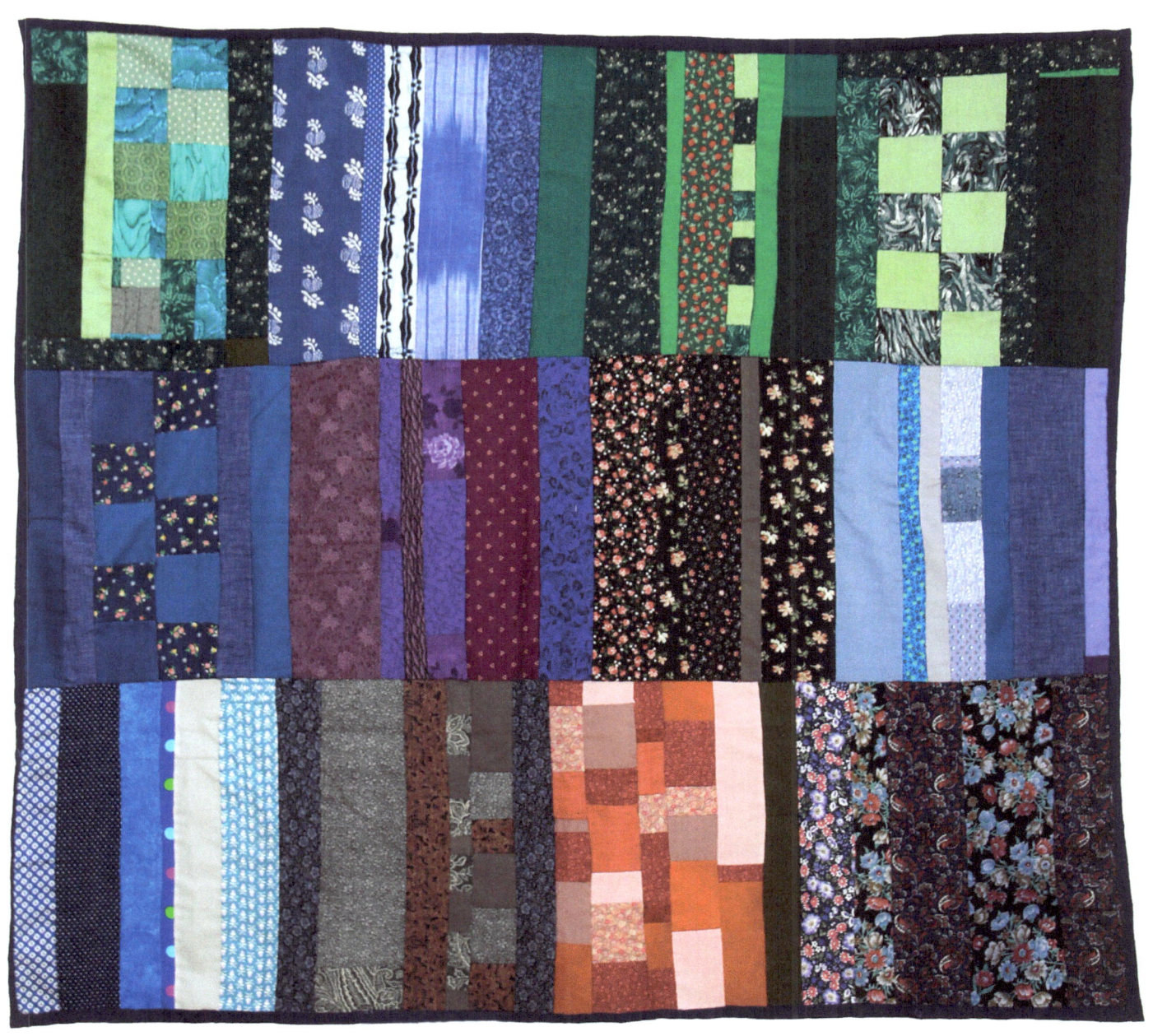

HOORAY FOR SATURDAY MARKET

Singing With Ernie,   2012
my Sweetheart and Valentine

Born on February 14, 1926

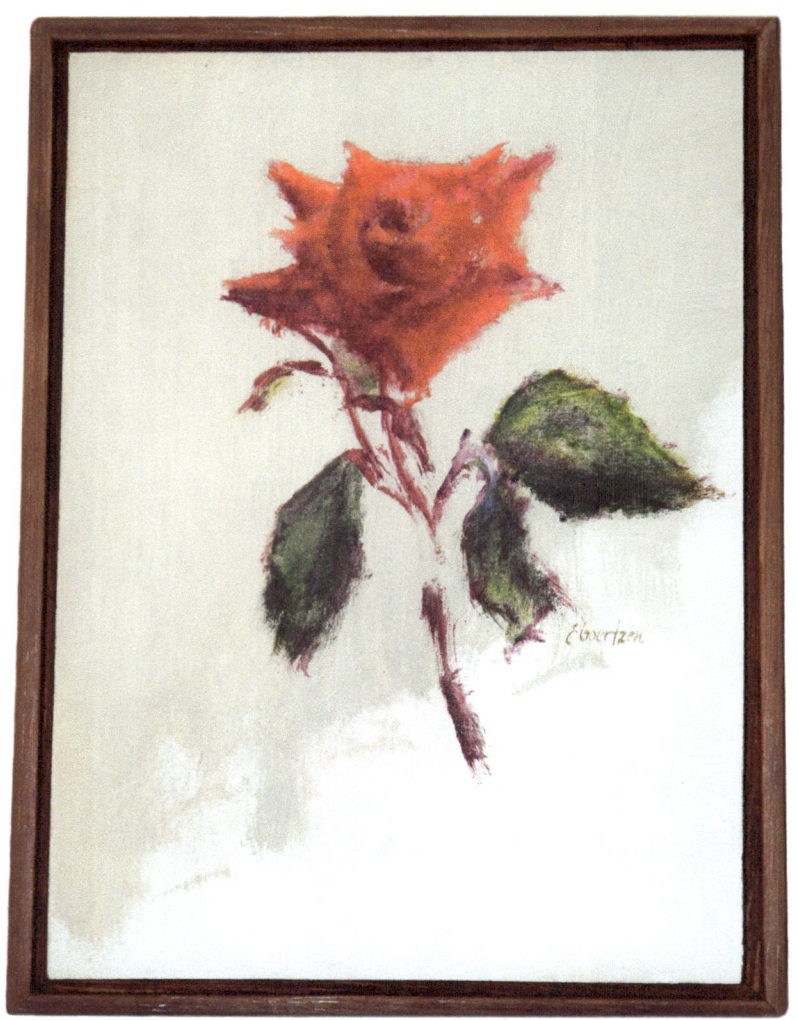

BY ERNIE GOERTZEN

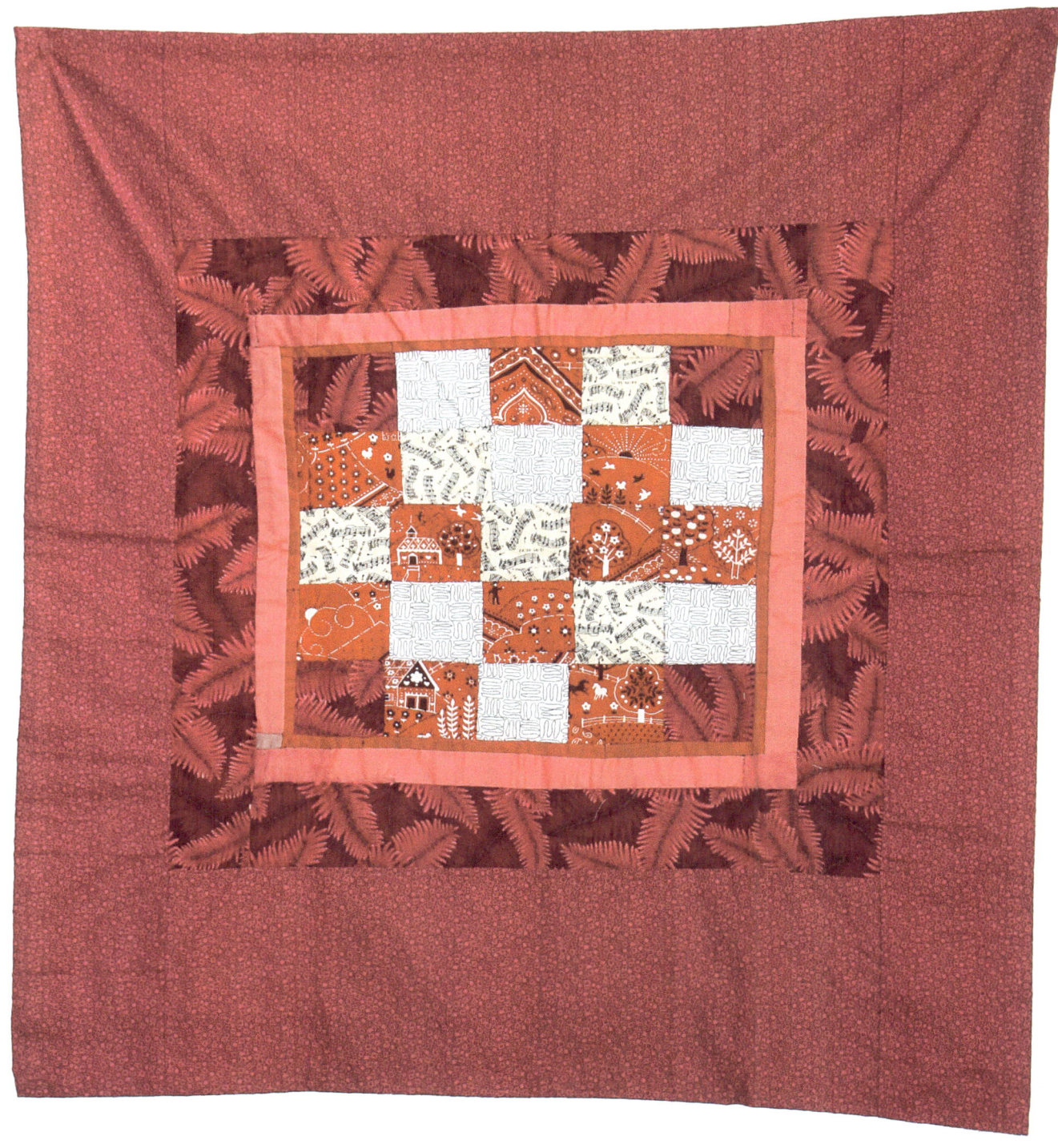

SINGING WITH ERNIE

I Come Home Singing 2012
in this sad world....
where one lover leaves
another, for all time, and
nothing to say with your
feet on the ground

words inspired by Natalie Goldberg

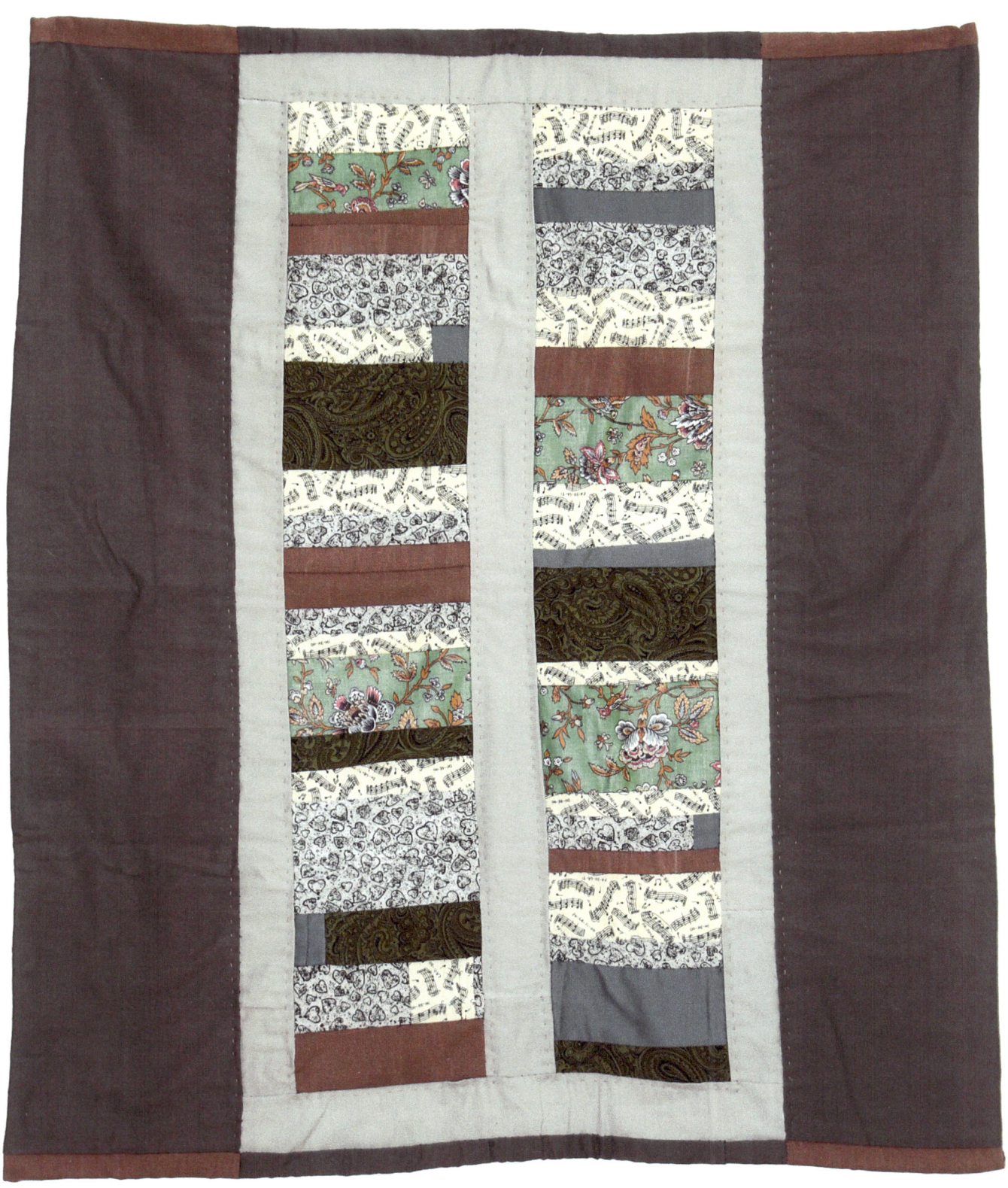

¡ COME HOME SINGING... IN THIS SAD WORLD

Grieving Quilt

I had a box of purple cloth that inspired me.

2012

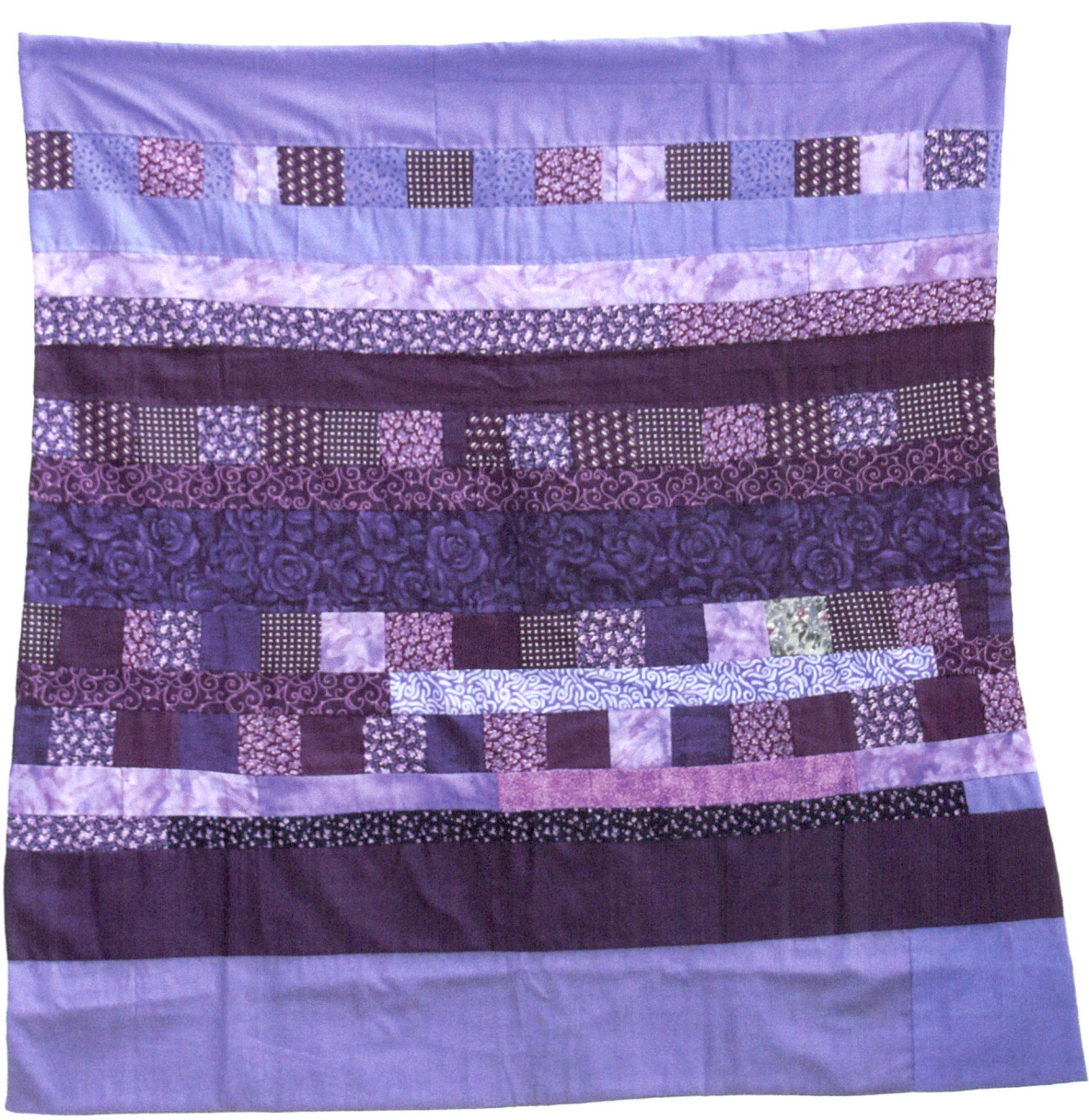

GRIEVING AFTER ERNIE DIED

I will venture into 2012
The darkness only as I
can carry fresh flowers.

Words inspired by my friend Pauline Thompson

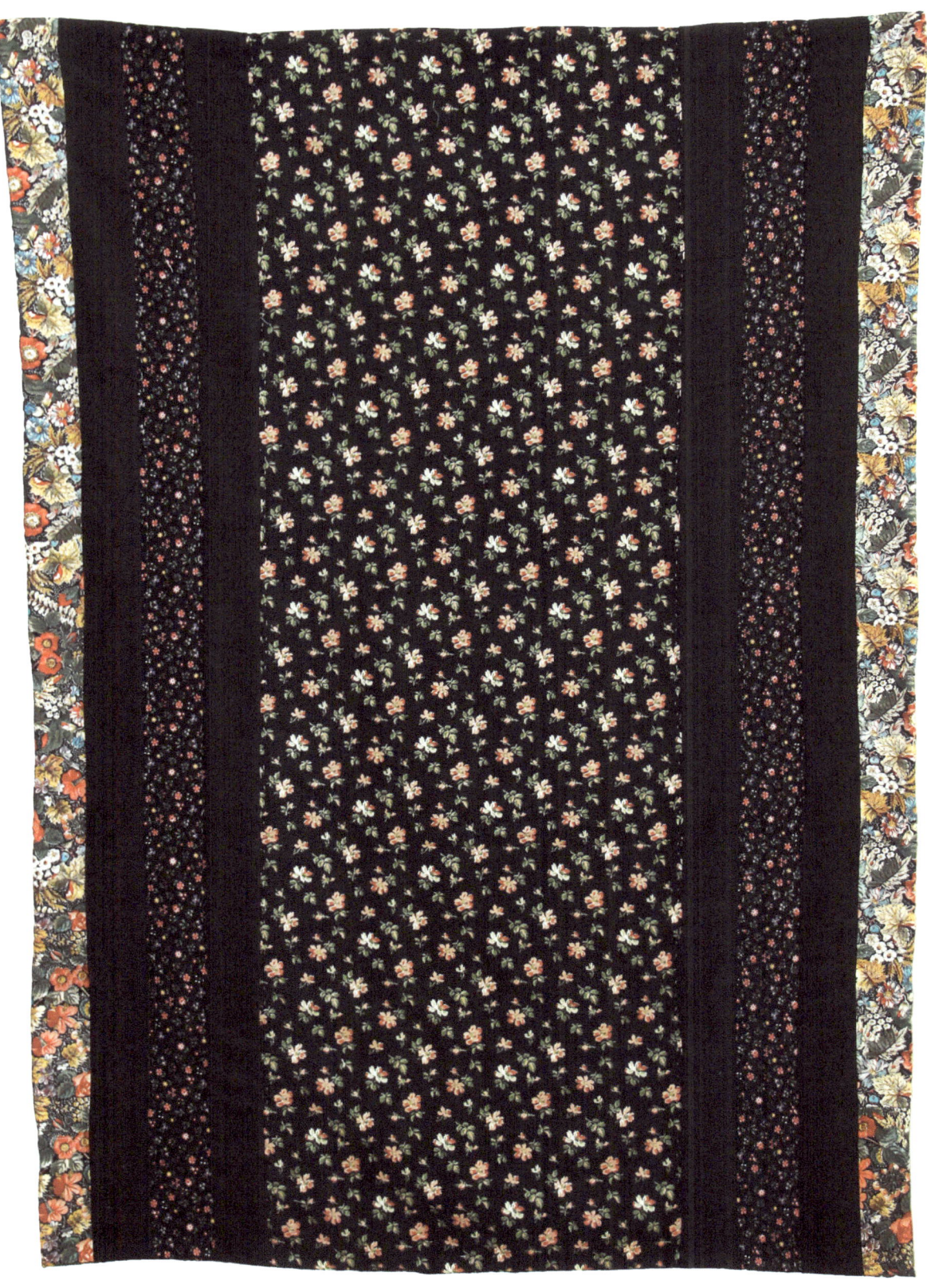

*I WILL VENTURE INTO THE DARKNESS ONLY AS FAR
AS I CAN CARRY FRESH FLOWERS*

2012

Nine White Foxgloves
on Ernie's grave July 3, 2008

In July of 2009 I
was opening the New and
Selected Poems by Mary Oliver
and noticed Ernie had penciled
on the title page 58 white
Flowers.

Some of the poem's words
described those white flowers
in a prophetic way - like
a message from Ernie with
white angel wings!

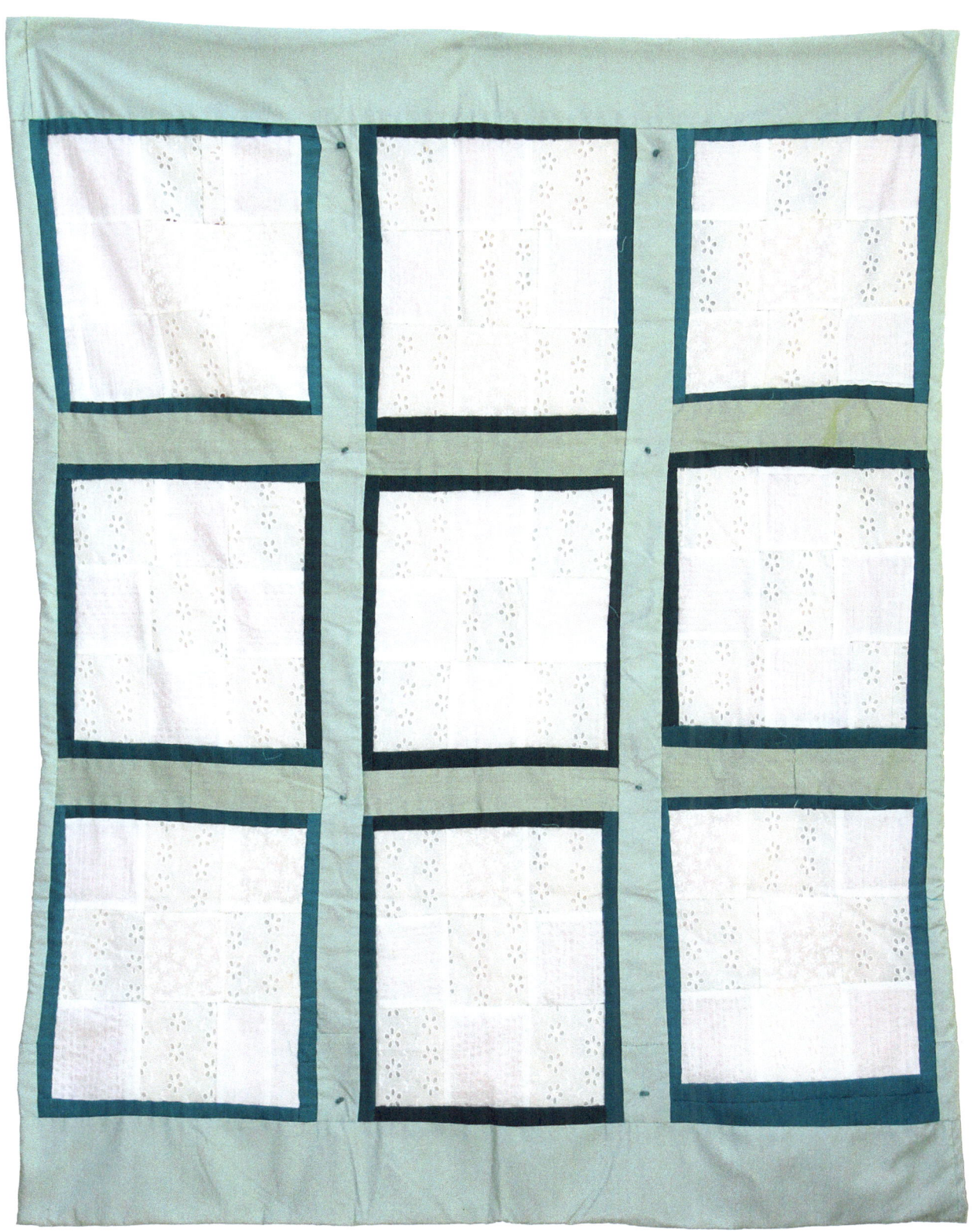

NINE WHITE FOXGLOVES ON ERNIE'S GRAVE

Gratefulness Quilt
2012

My favorite colors,
Green and blue
earth and sky

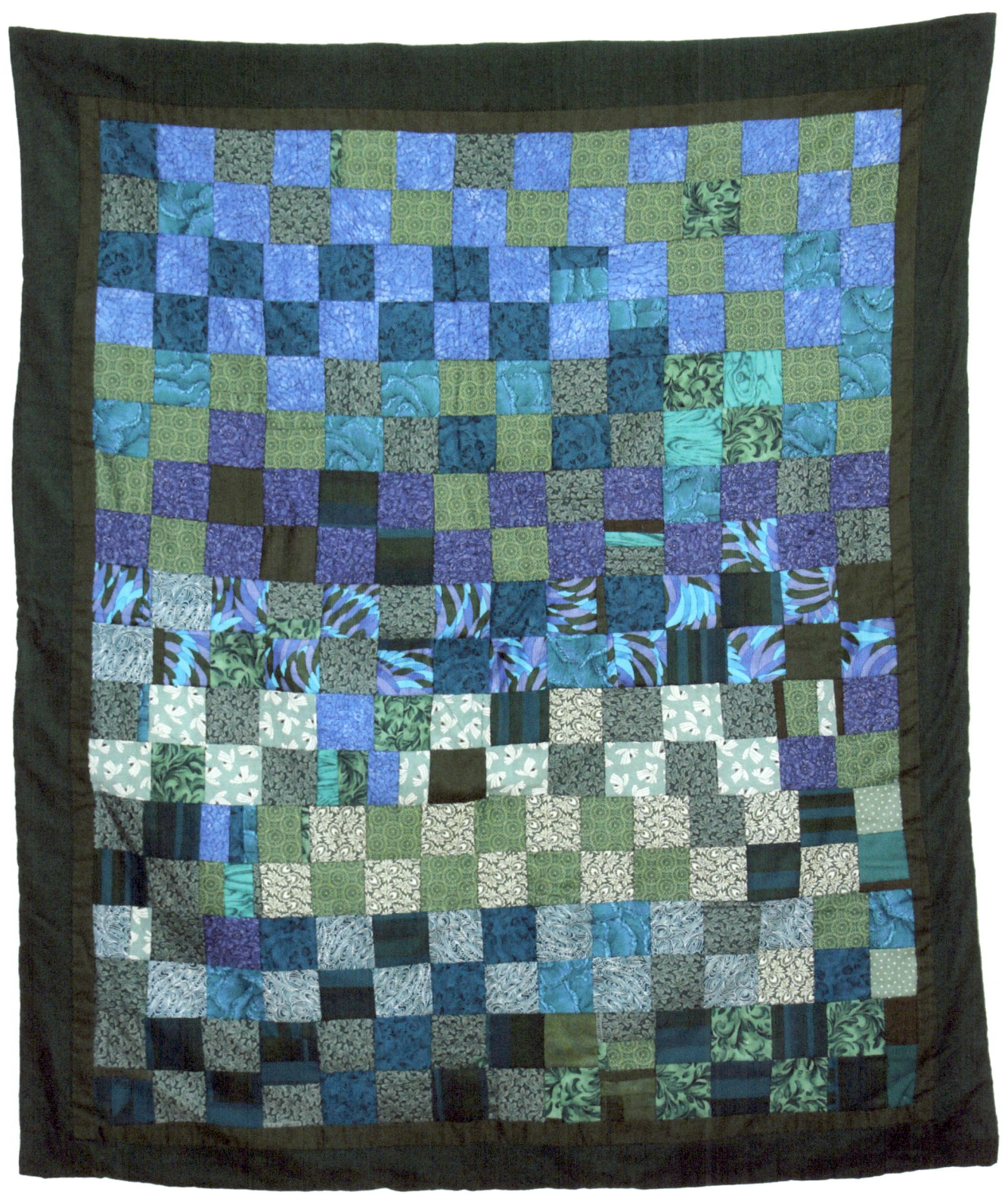

GRATEFULNESS QUILT

Old Fashioned Joyful with warm colors and flowers

2012

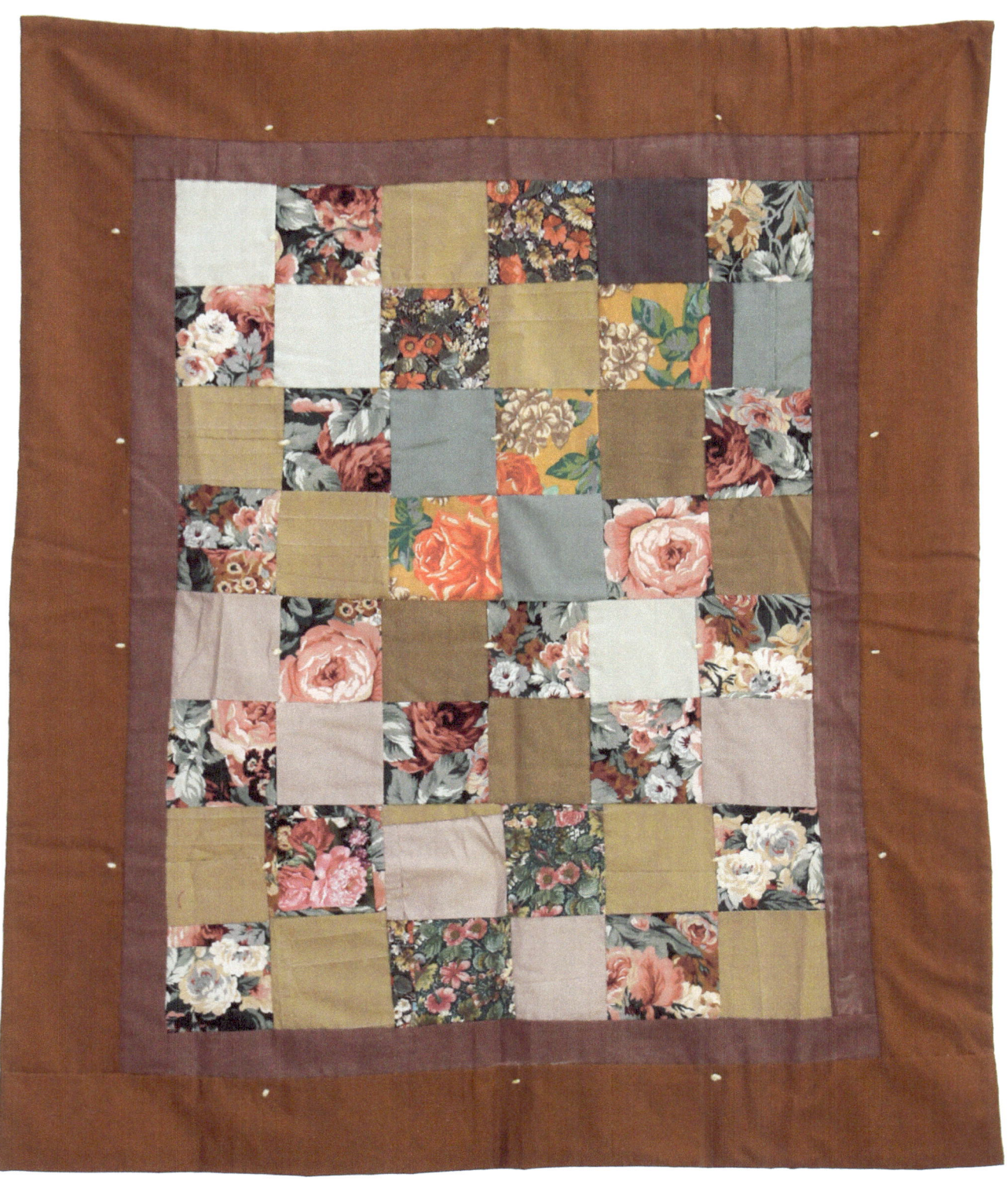

OLD FASHIONED JOYFUL

Singing
" This little light of mine,
I'm gonna let it shine "

2013

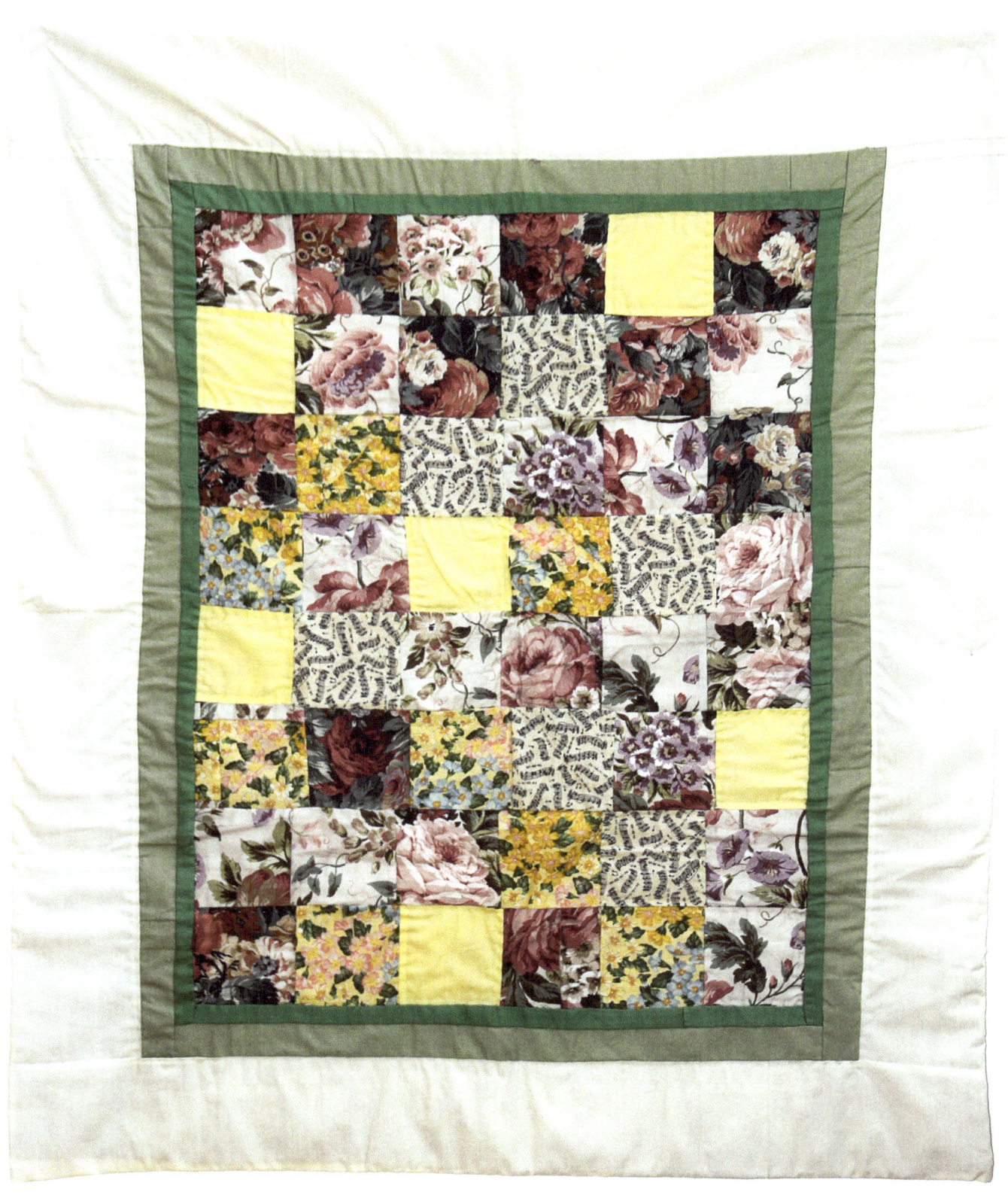

SINGING "THIS LITTLE LIGHT OF MINE"

Listening to the Radio
2012

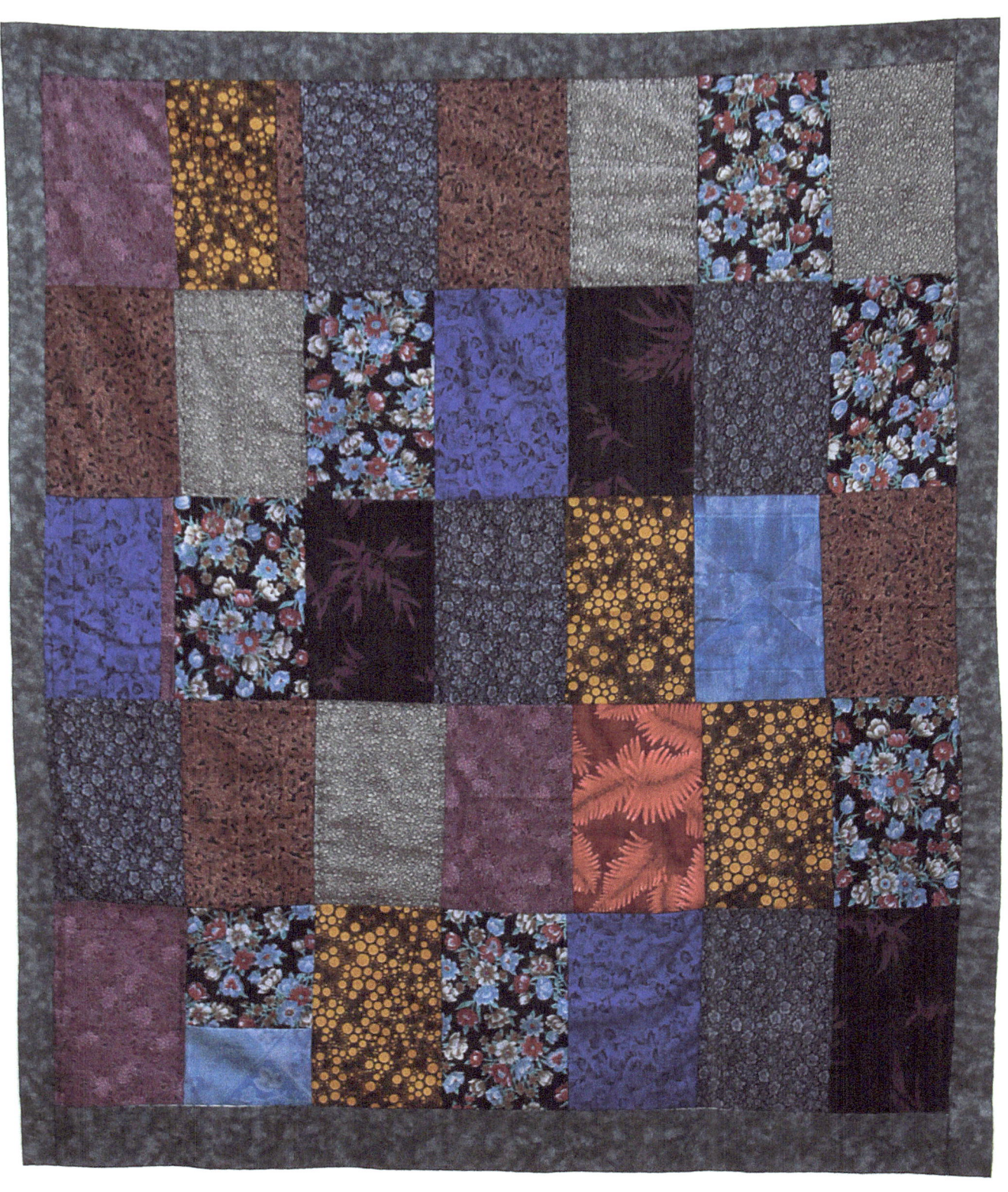

LISTENING TO THE RADIO

Thomas Merton's comment about the utter nonsense of everything and laughing and laughing with the sky and the trees prompted this quilt which I made while listening to the three presidential debates and the one vice-presidential debate.

2012

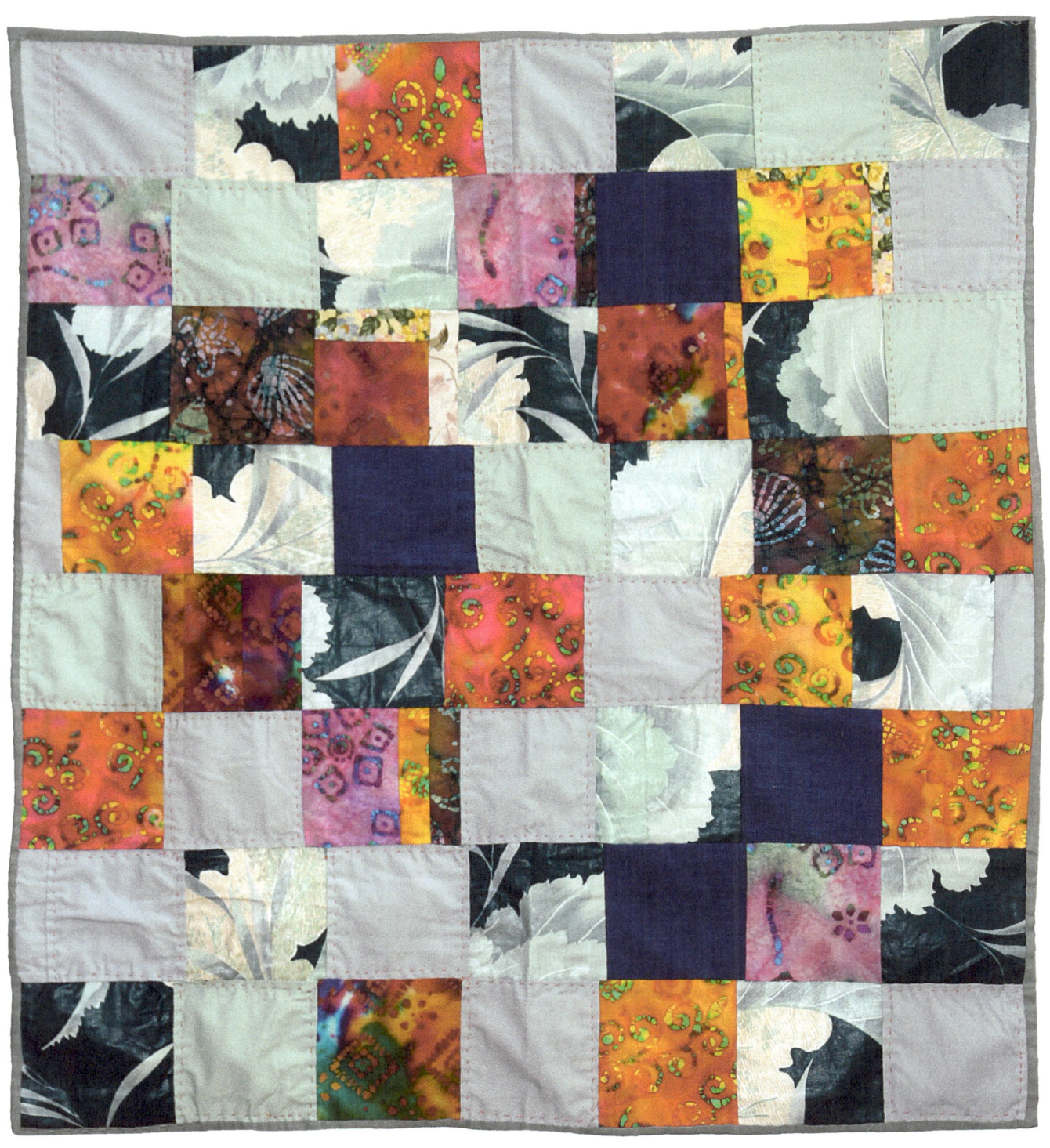

THE UTTER NONSENSE OF EVERYTHING

Inspired by a
Rumi poem
about meeting you
in a field out
beyond ideas of
wrongdoing and
right doing.
2013

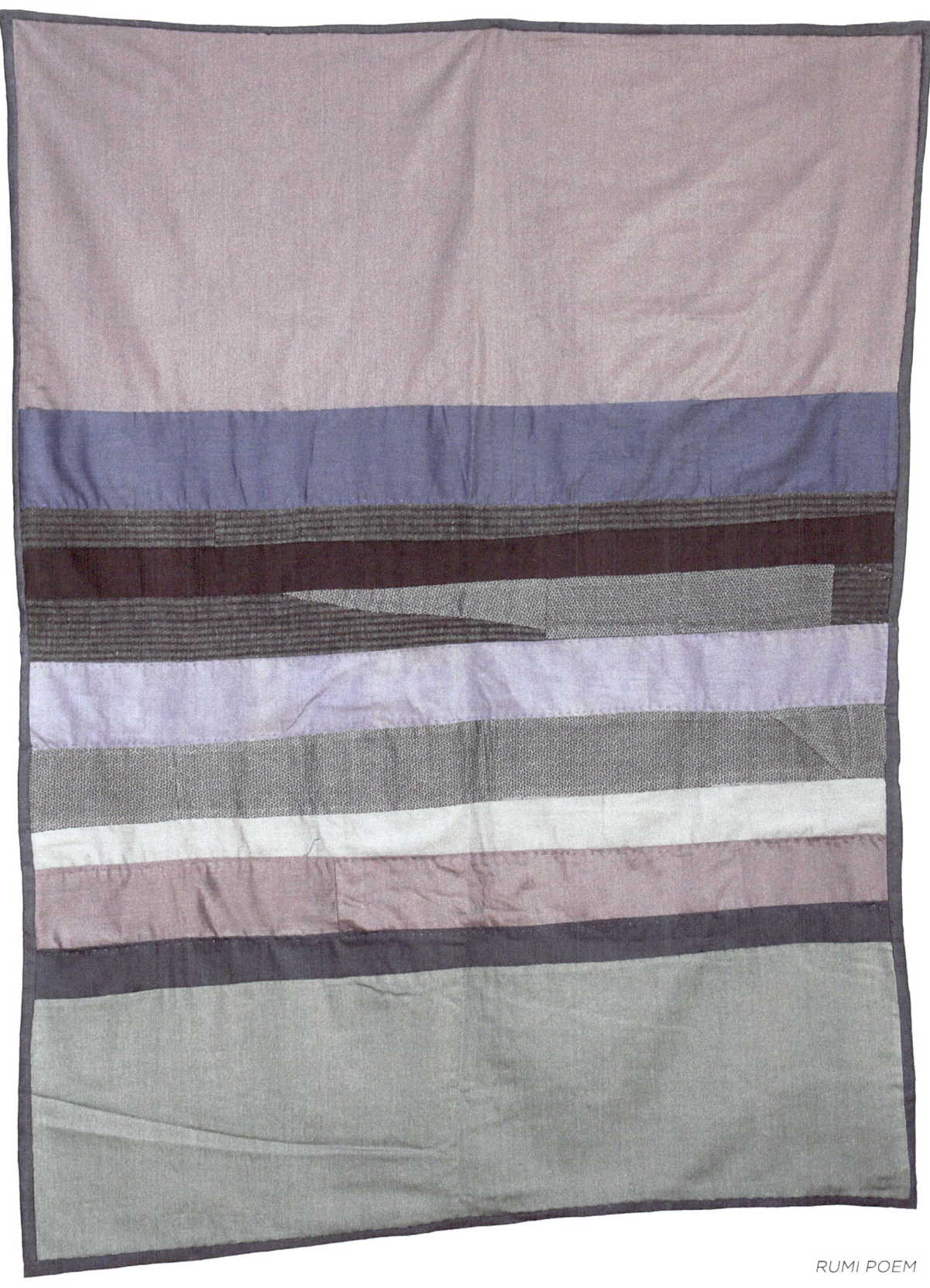

RUMI POEM

Canfield Family

Celebrating our years of family
times together — in Kansas
and Berkeley   2013

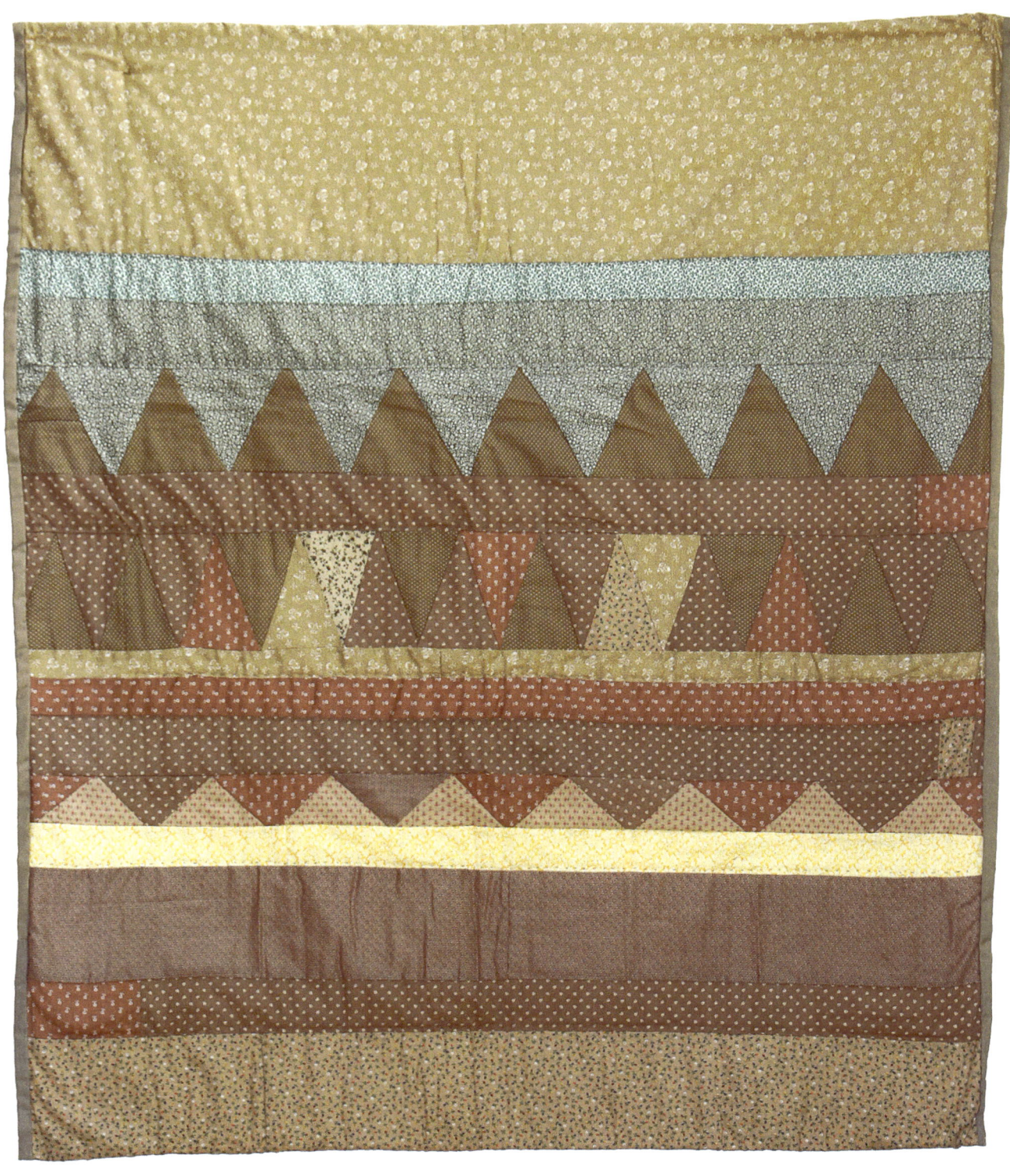

*CELEBRATING OUR FRIENDSHIP WITH
THE KANSAS CANFIELD FAMILY*

Yoshiko,
a special friendship
2013

Our children were similar
ages and we had many family
times together in Berkeley
days and beyond.

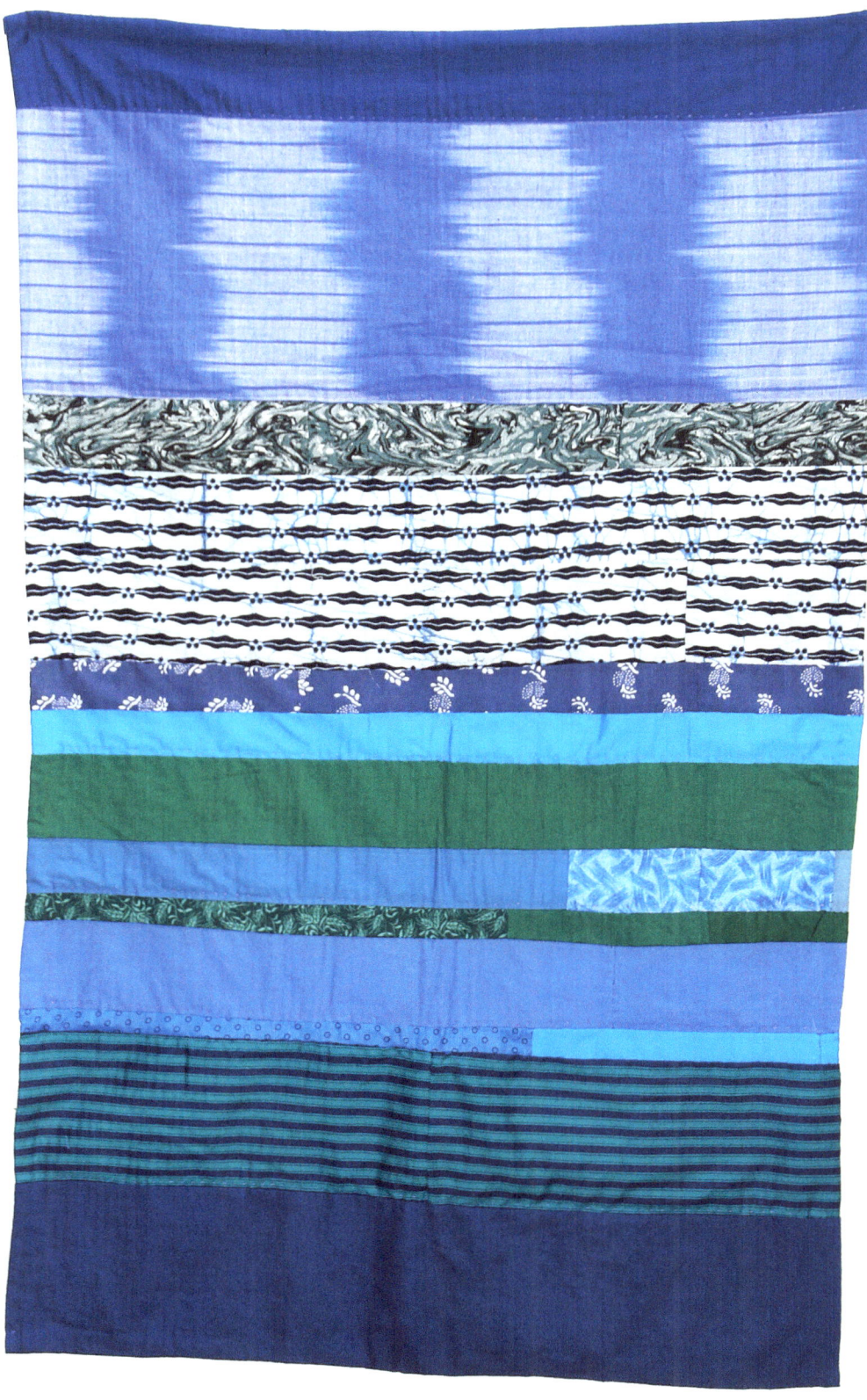

FOR YOSHIKO

Jimmy, Iky and Eldie

In honore of my brother
and his two childhood buddies

2013

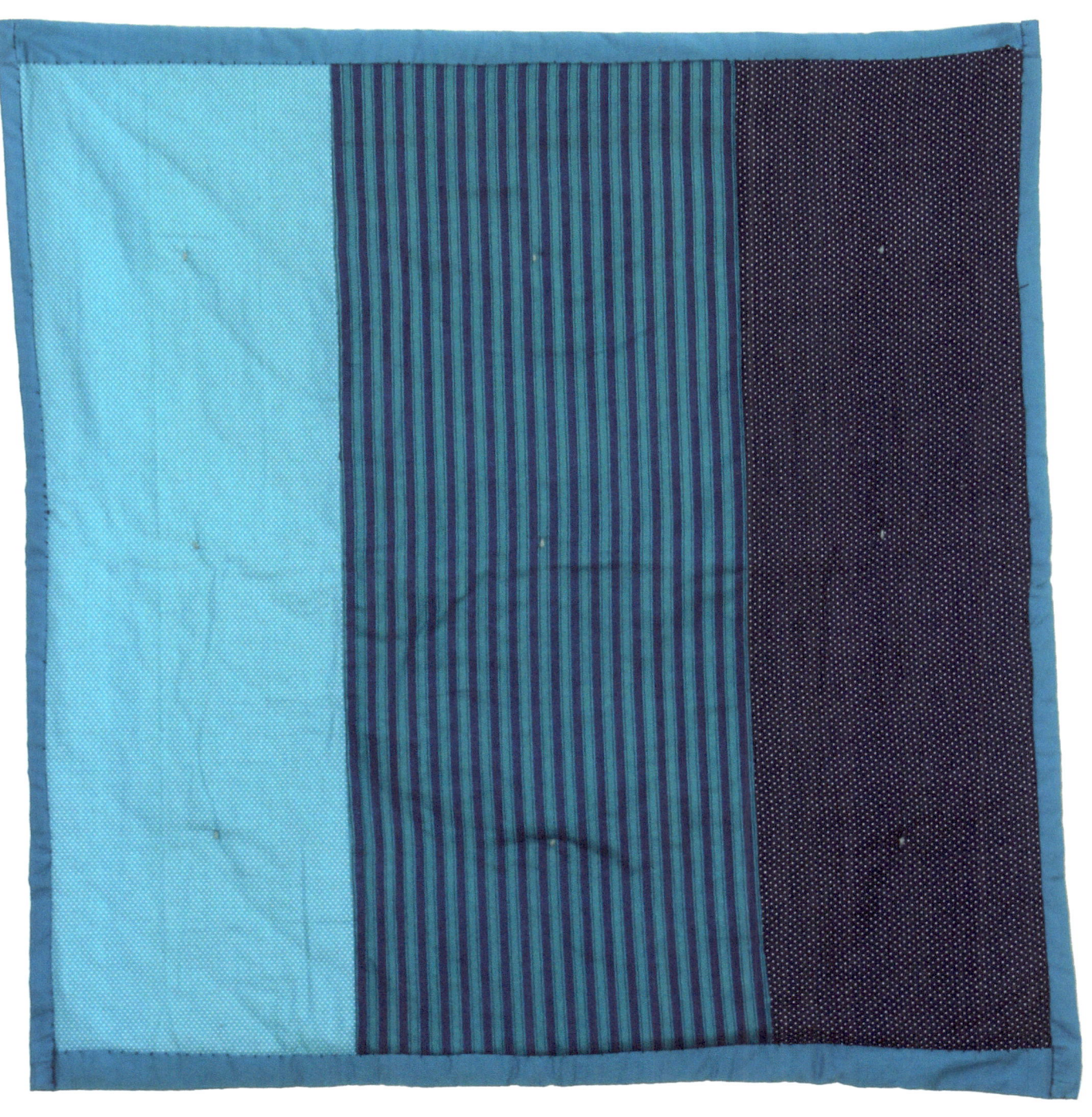

JIMMY, IKY AND ELDIE

My cat, Reno   2013

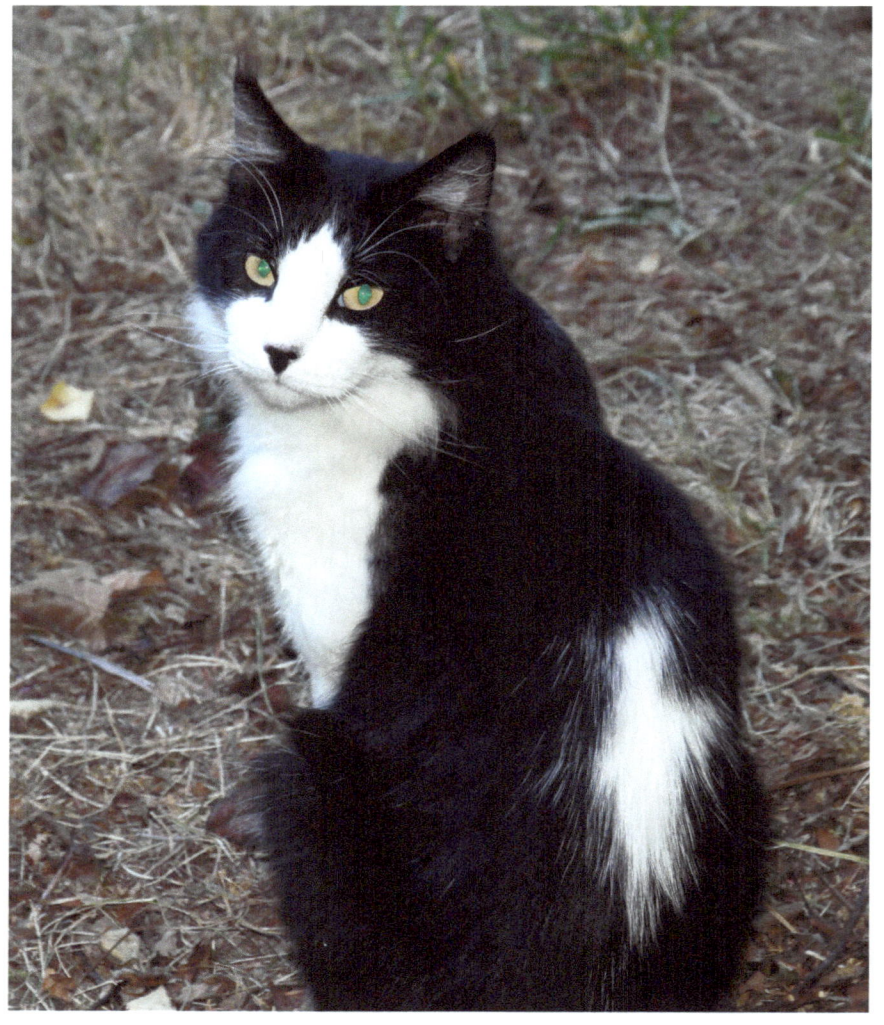

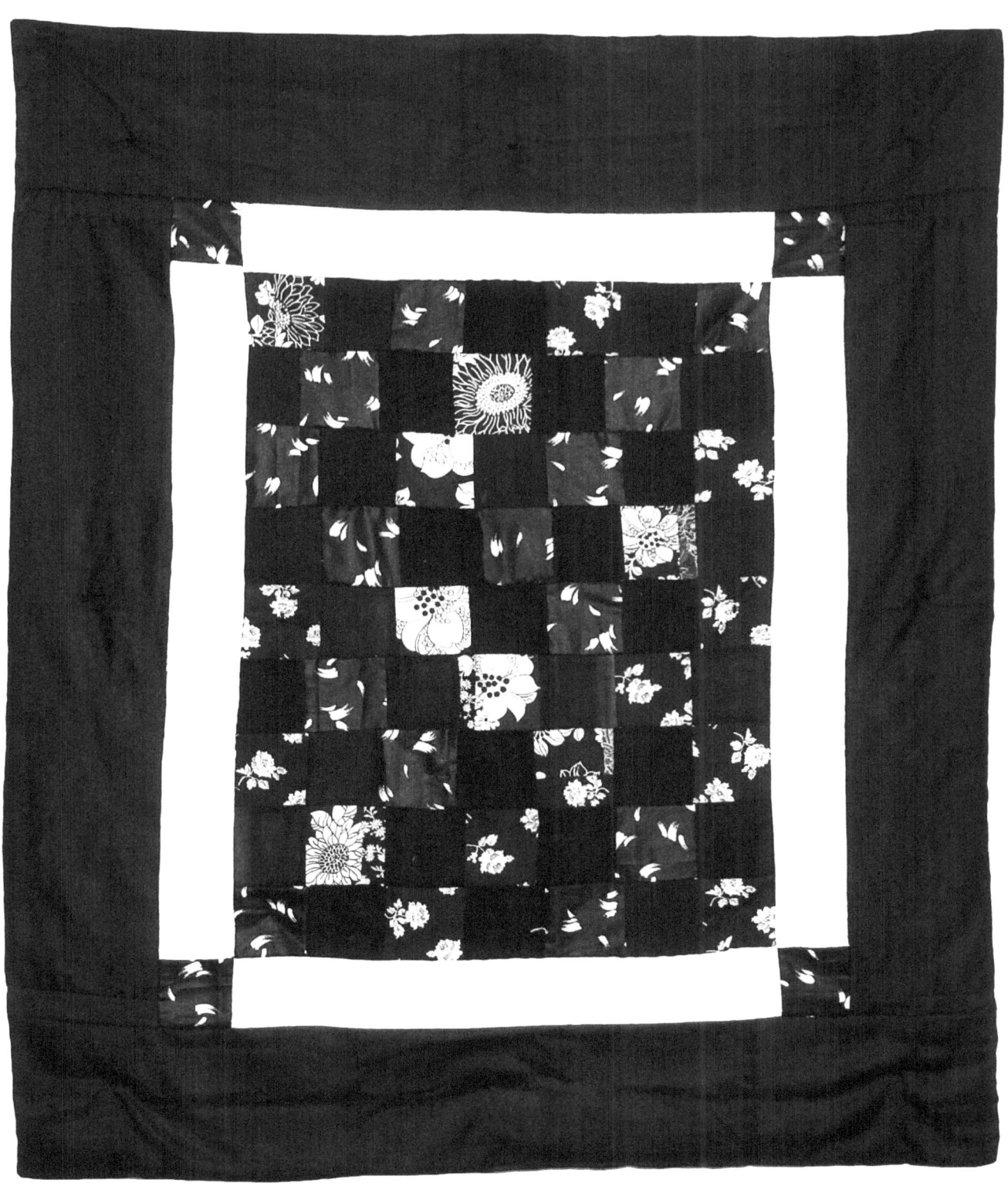

MY CAT, RENO

One day at a time and each day is different

2013

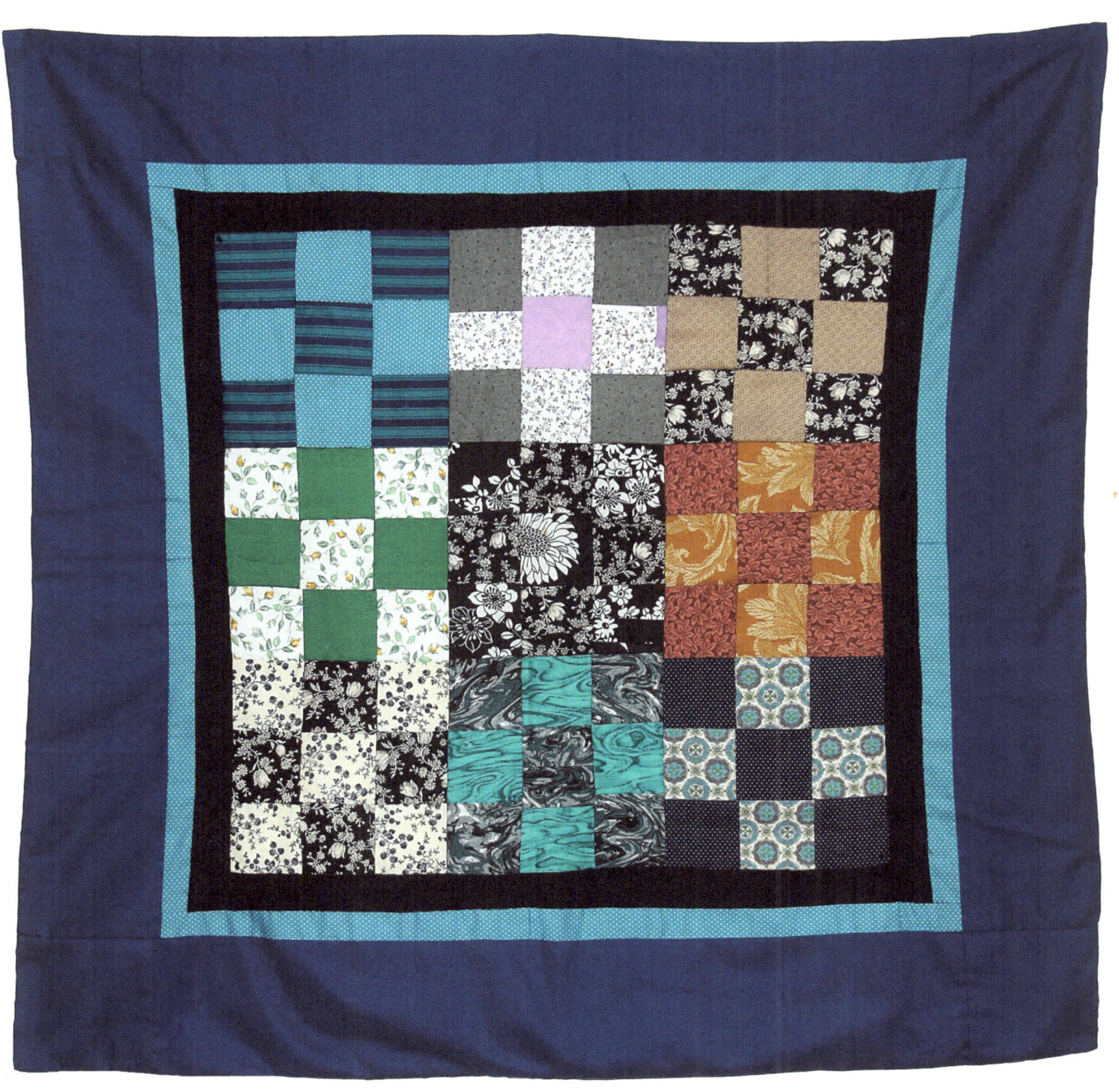

ONE DAY AT A TIME

In touch with my moods
Some days larger than others
The border a surprising touch

2013

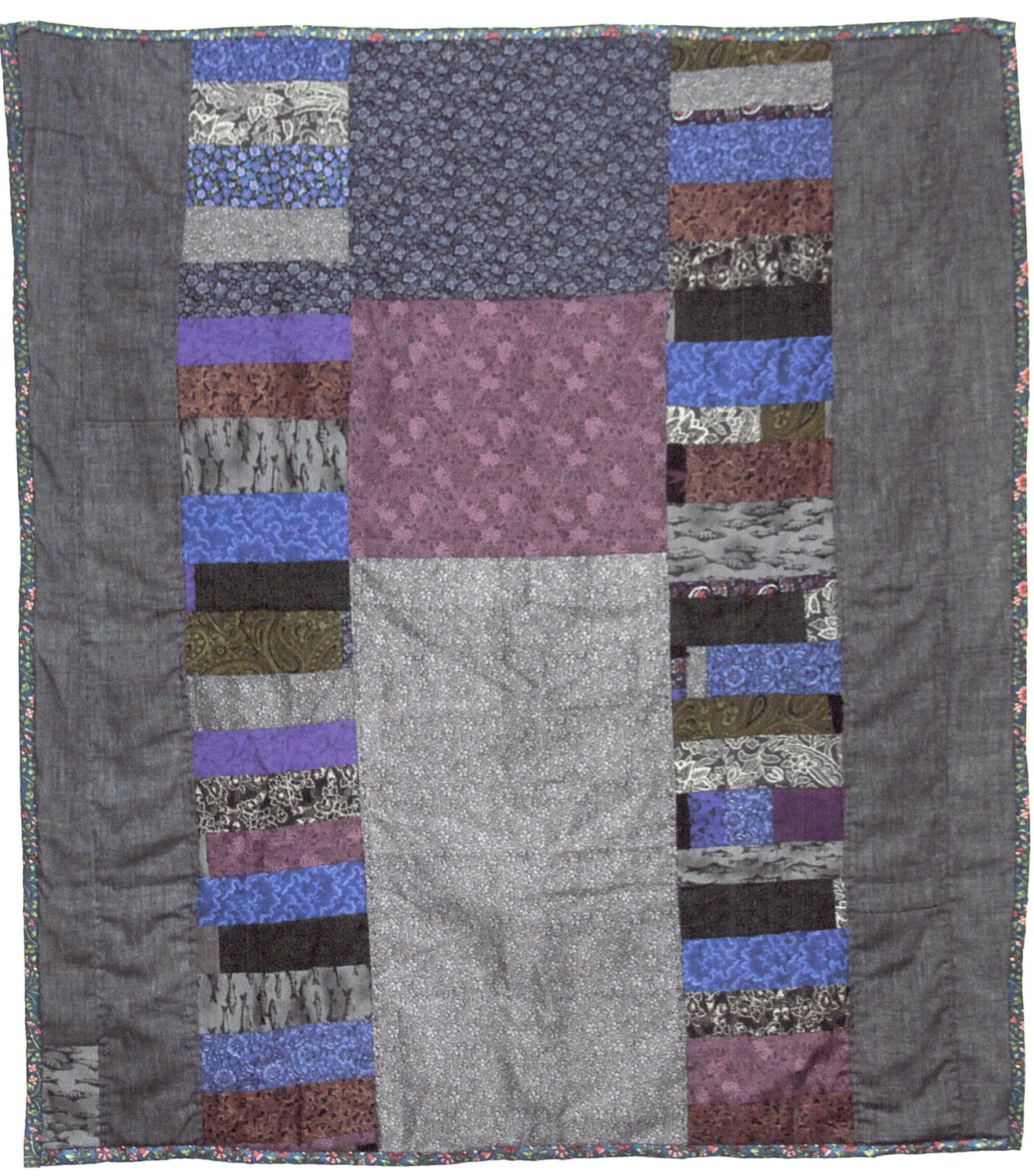

IN TOUCH WITH MY MOODS

Living in the Now
One day at a time
The future will unfold

2012
Made during son David's spinal
surgery — every stitch a prayer

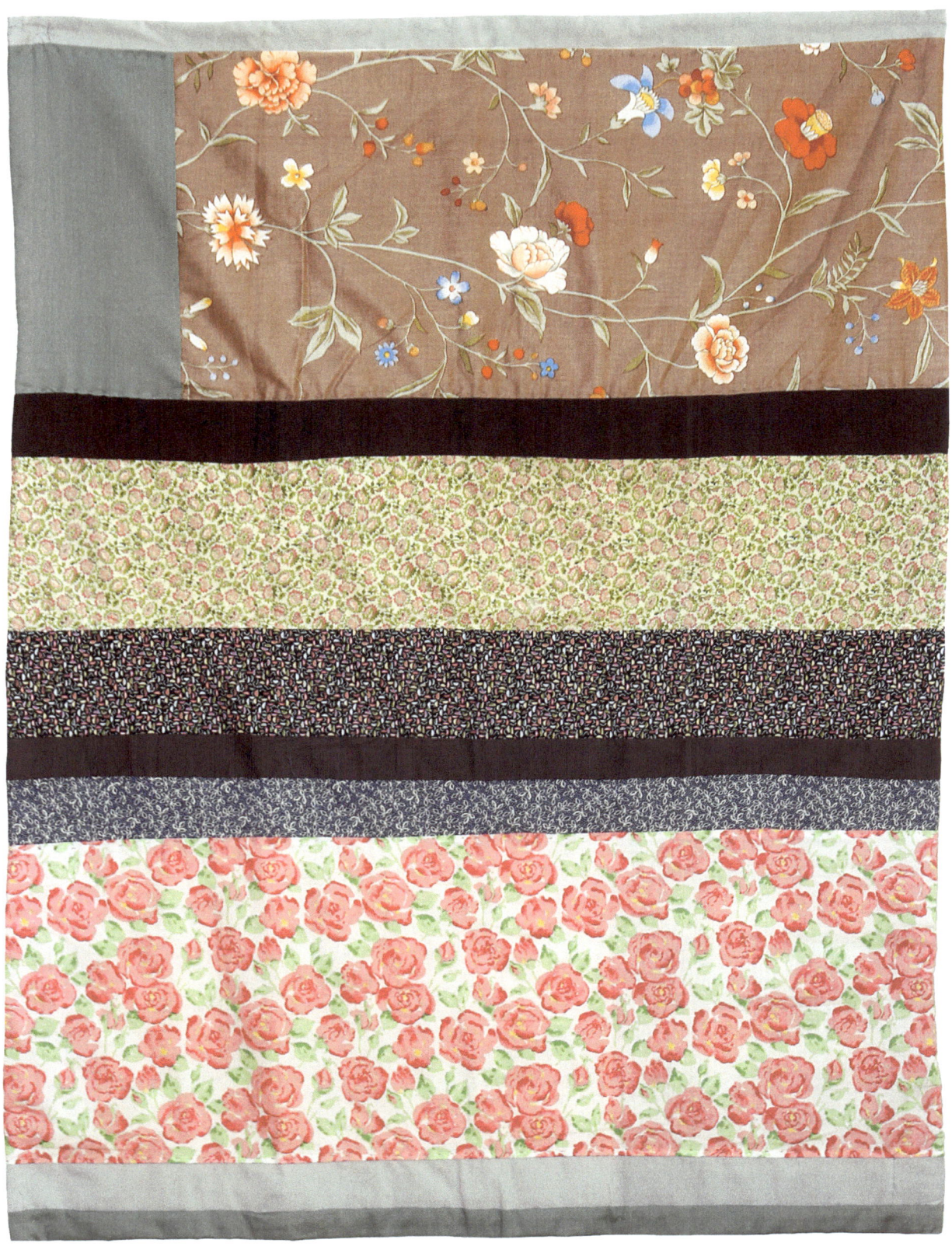

LIVING IN THE NOW

Inspired by friend and
neighbor, Maryanne
2013

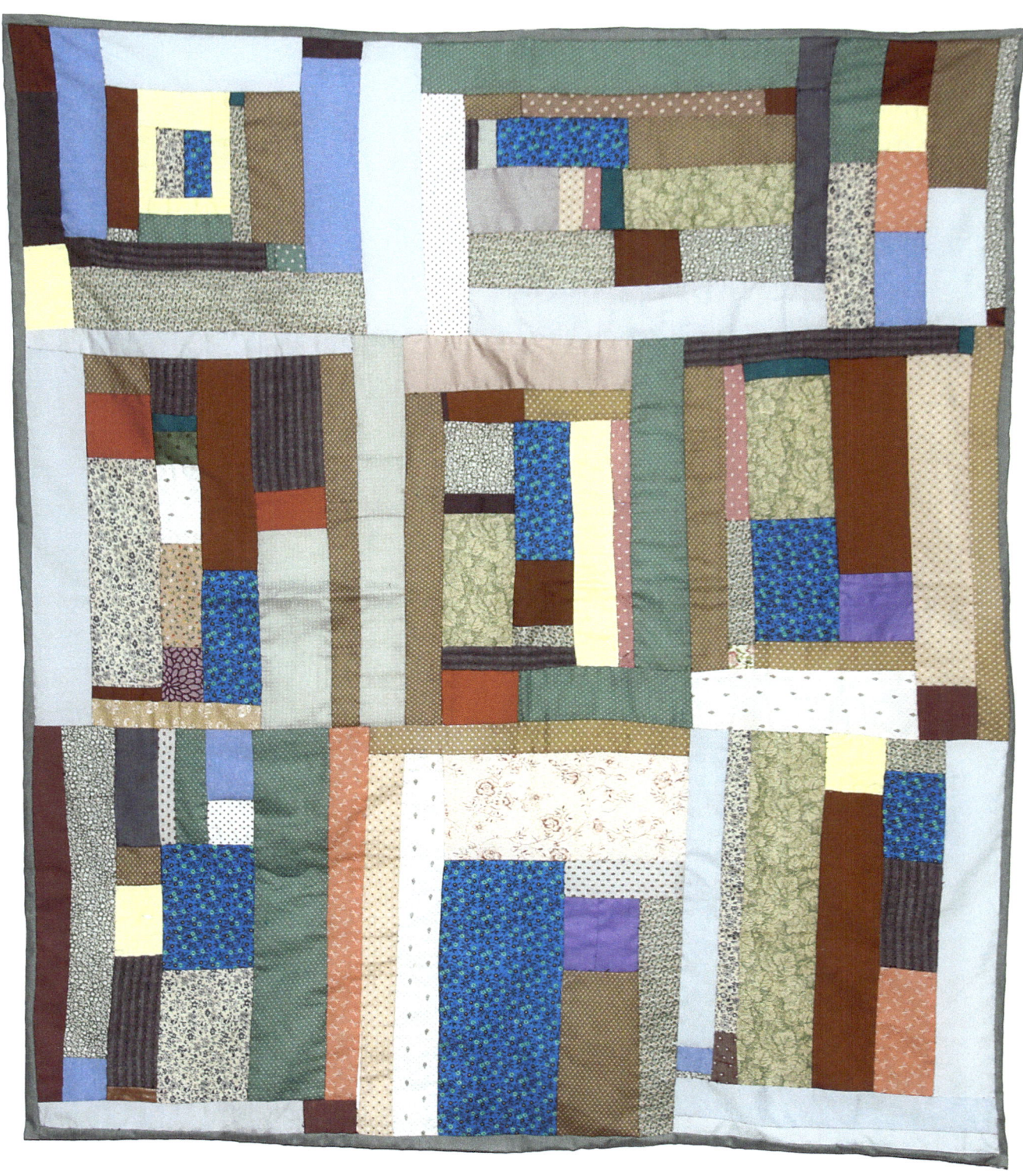

THANKS, FRIEND MARY ANNE

Housetop quilt pattern
Inspired by
    Pees Bend Quilters
It seemed to make itself
                    2013

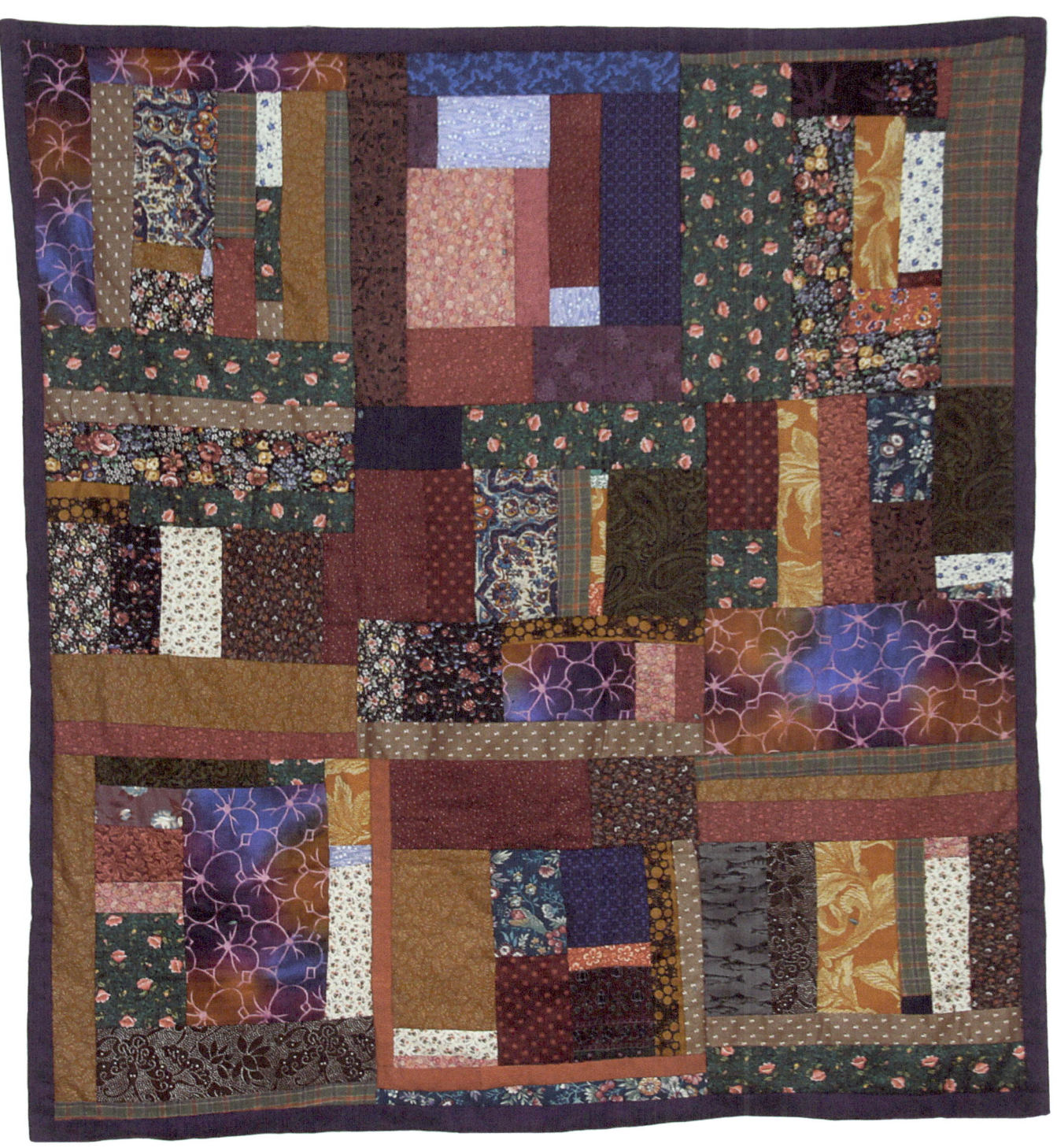

INSPIRED BY GEE'S BEND

Enjoying the cloth
with very little cutting
2013

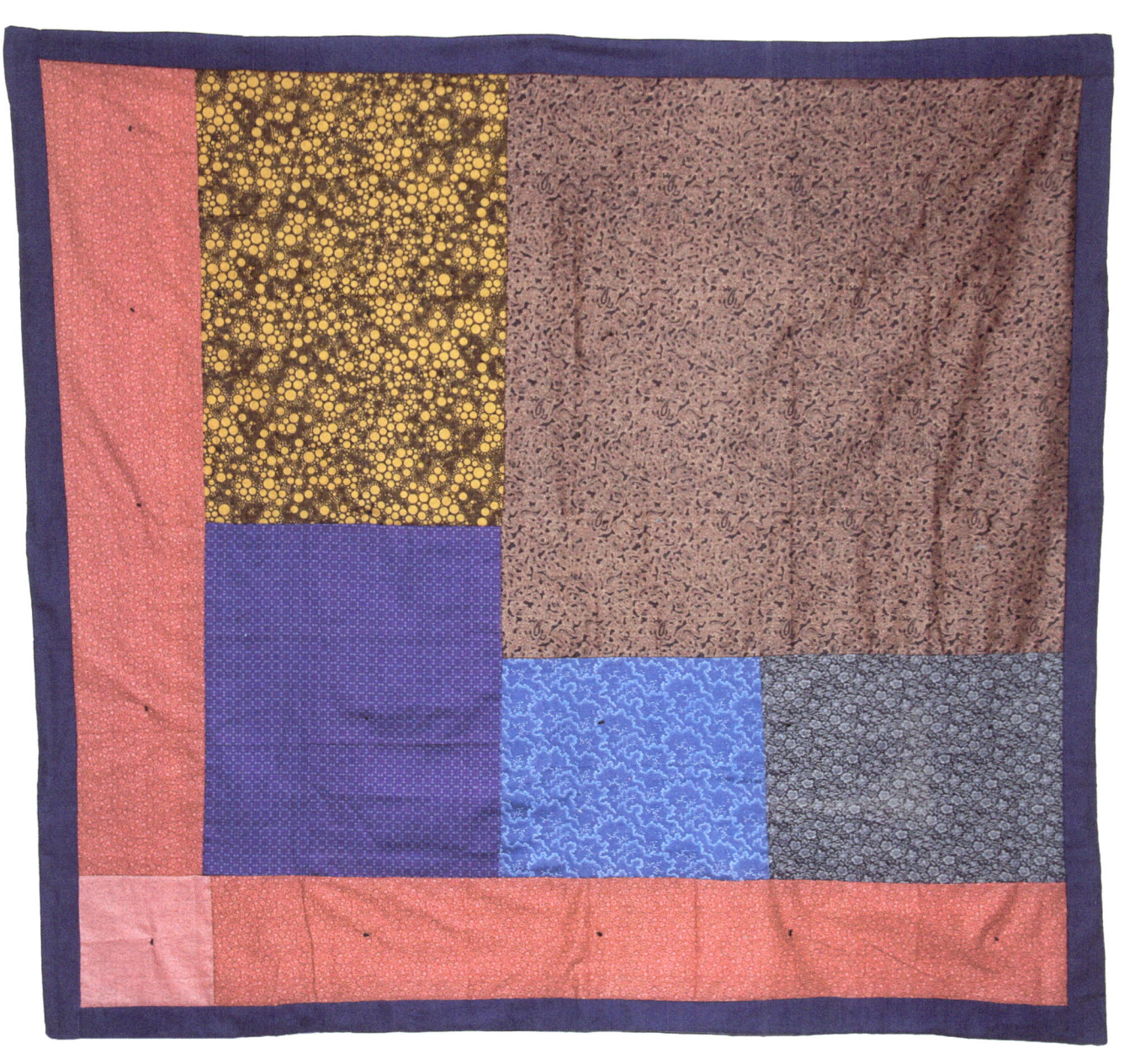

ENJOYING THE CLOTH

About the Artist

Mary Lou Goertzen, born in 1929, grew up on the Mennonite Bethel College campus in North Newton, Kansas.

She and her husband, Ernie, married after they graduated from Bethel College in 1951 and then taught school in western Kansas and Nebraska.

In 1965 they moved to Berkeley, California where they sold their paintings in outdoor art shows.

In 1975 they moved to Deadwood, Oregon and continued selling their artwork at the Eugene Saturday Market.

Mary Lou's flower drawings were also being published by Portal Publications and she then designed Block China dinnerware from 1980 to 1990.

After that, the quilt making era began.

To contact Mary Lou, please address correspondence to Mary Lou Goertzen, Deadwood, OR 97430. For more information about Mary Lou, please visit www.marylougoertzen.com.

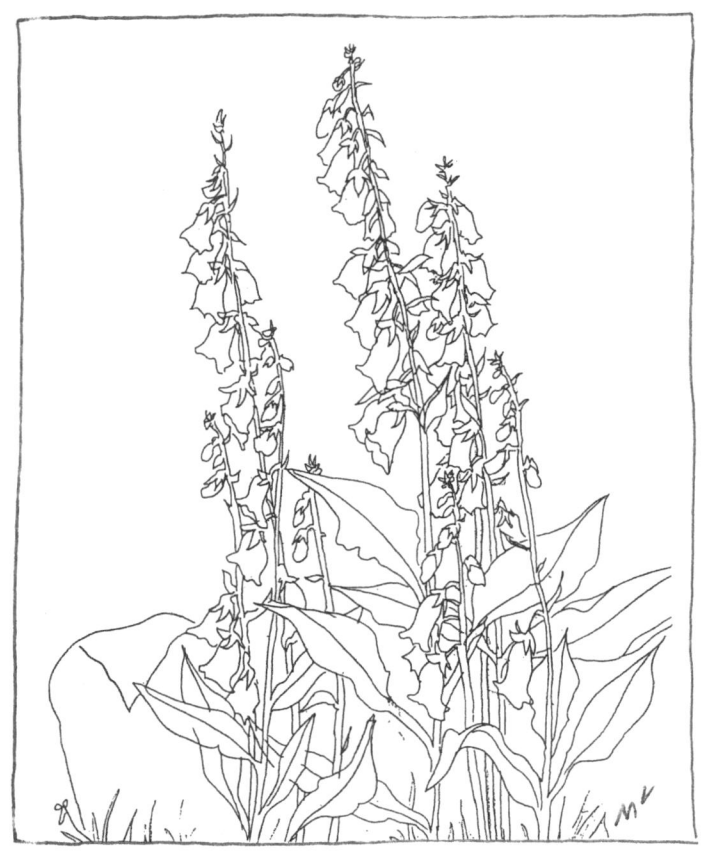

WHITE FOXGLOVES ON ERNIE'S GRAVE, JULY 2008

www.ingramcontent.com/pod-product-compliance
Lightning Source LLC
Chambersburg PA
CBHW040744200526
45159CB00023B/1688